Passing the 70 Plus

Sylvia Downs
Trish Perry

First Printed in 2009

downs publications
2 Jerviston Gardens
London
SW16 3EL

© Sylvia Downs, 2009
Illustrations by Trish Perry

British Library Cataloguing in Publication Data
A record of this book is available from the British Library
ISBN 987-0-9561353-1-5

Printed and bound in Great Britain by Think Ink

Acknowledgements

Our thanks to many people, often from formal groups, who shared their ideas and experiences with us.

Thank you also to the publishers for their patience, and enthusiasm.

Contents

Passing the 70 Plus

This is a book about being over 70 years old. It is divided roughly into three sections, ending, as it should, on a positive note with the benefits. It begins with a section about forgetting, or rather, what people do to help them remember. Following this is a collection of ways that people have found helpful in dealing with some of the other effects of getting older, such as how to exercise.

The book has been put together from experiences, both positive and negative, of people over 70 years old, with the actions they took to counter any ill effects and make the most of the good.

Illustrations have been used to make the points, rather than lengthy verbal descriptions. Equally, by coupling amusement with the point being made, the message tends to be more easily remembered.

Forgotten Something?

Lapses of memory affect everyone, particularly, it seems, as they get older. "Where did I put my glasses?", "What **was** that person's name?" and "what have I come upstairs for?", are just examples of familiar memory lapses.

This section describes some ways that people have found helpful in overcoming or avoiding forgetfulness. Many of them you may well know and practise, while there could be some that are worth trying or perhaps even trying again.

Make notes on post-its and leave them in obvious places.

JUDITH WONDERED HOW SHE EVER
MANAGED WITHOUT "NOTELETS"

Label everything you can,
such as jars, tins, and boxes.

Use pill boxes with separate parts for each day of the week and put your regular pills in at the start of each week.

Get a digital clock that also tells you the day of the week and the date.

When carrying belongings, e.g. handbag, umbrella, and luggage, count how many things you are taking and after stopping anywhere count again.

Never leave the house without checking you have your keys. Have an emergency set somewhere easy to get at.

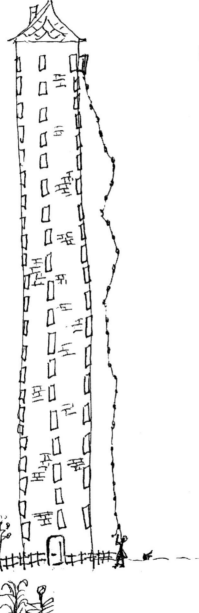

It's amazing
what you
can do with
an extending
pole.!!

As well as shopping lists, write Christmas lists and daily lists to help you sort out your time.

Check what you are wearing before you go out, e.g. have you got your slippers on?

Link people's names with as many associations as you can, especially funny ones or naughty ones. Keep repeating names as much as possible.

A church minister talked about the "hereafter". When you go into a room, ask "what am I here after".

When you have to do things in
a sequence number them.

If you remember
anything that needs action,
DO IT AT ONCE

FRED SHAKES HIS MEDICINE

If you want to take something with you put it by the door.

Get a blank wall chart for a year and write in all the birthdays and anniversaries. Also write in year of birth of grandchildren to help remember how old they are.

Do not get frustrated
when you forget;
everyone forgets sometimes.

Have a big blank calendar
to record activities,
and check it frequently.

What Helped Other 70 Plus People?

The second section is a mixture of attitudes, physical factors and mental activity. The last word, "activity" is the centrepiece to most of the suggestions that were made by the contributors and to quote an old saying "If you don't use it you lose it".

What was often implied was that a positive mind set is very important in avoiding the trap of self pity or gloominess. For example, one of the suggestions was to distinguish between loneliness and aloneness and learn to treasure the latter.

One of the commonest
problems when people get
older is to trip and fall.
Research has shown that the
best way to prevent this
is to train oneself
to put one's foot down
heel first then toe.

"If you have not got an alarm
call pendant then take your
mobile phone with you
when gardening".

An older woman living in a flat accessed by stairs said, "When I come down stairs to get my post I go down, up, down and up again, I'm 92 and I need to make sure I keep fit".

Don't be sentimental about possessions. If the old family furniture is too big for a modern flat give it to the family, sell it or give it away. They are only things.

"When getting out of my shower, I stepped out with one foot and slipped badly falling on my other foot. Now I get out of the shower backwards, while holding on. This keeps my centre of gravity in the shower until I am stable on the floor.

VENUS ARISES BACKWARDS
NOW SHE IS MATURE

"I am 80 years old, an ex heavy truck driver and I had a stroke some time ago so can't be so active, I measured my corridor, it's 9 yards long – I make sure I walk that several times a day to keep fit."

Discussing problems with a close friend or trustworthy neighbour (avoid gossips) usually ends in laughter and the shared problem feels less threatening.

If there is a real problem
then discuss it with
someone you trust and
then if necessary get
professional advice.
Don't just ignore it.

SHARING THOUGHTS IS
REWARDING

Realise there is a difference between aloneness and loneliness and learn to cherish aloneness – this helps long term after bereavement.

BORIS TOOK HIS
RIVER DANCING
VERY SERIOUSLY

— AND HE DIDN'T
NEED A PARTNER

When you are feeling low just identify the small real things that you really enjoy, and concentrate on them.

"I keep a basket at the top
and bottom of the stairs.
I fill it with items to go up or
down, to save a journey."

Don't give advice
unless asked. Remember
an elderly 'know it all'
is a pain in the posterior.

DON'T SHARE YOUR KNOWLEDGE
TOO READILY WITH YOUNGER
PEOPLE

Enjoy your money, however small. Do not feel guilty about having treats, dress as stylishly as you can afford. Wear a red hat if you want to.

Make choices while you are still able. Don't put off moving from a big old property until you can no longer cope with the house and garden.

Having problems climbing in
and out of a car? Put a plastic
bag on the seat and sit on it,
then swing your legs in.
Put on your seat belt to
stop you slipping forward.

Remember that our grandchildren are their parents' responsibility, not ours. Don't feel put out if you are not consulted.

Get a pick up stick to get things from the ground.

HORACE FOUND HIS
NEW PICK UP STICK
VERY USEFUL
AFTER MAUREEN'S
GIRLIE EVENING

Avoid having mats around the house; fewer mats mean fewer trips.

Do a mind exercise each day,
such as puzzles or crosswords.

Avoid sitting too long.
Get up and do something that
involves a change of position,
such as tidying a drawer,
sorting something in a
cupboard or filing photos.

HENRY THOUGHT DORIS ASKED HIM TO
PLAY 'POOL' NOT PLAY 'IN THE POOL'

It is important to speak
regularly with others.

If you can, get a pet,
such as a bird.

Rubbing cream on the small of your back with the back of your hand makes it easier to reach further.

Relax and Enjoy Your Success

Having reached the age of 70, most of you are no longer responsible for raising families. So now you can think about yourself and relax a bit. Others help because the general public expect the older members to take things a bit easy and not to try to change the world.

This does not mean that all responsibilities are cast away. Grandchildren can be looked after, but then handed back, so that responsibilities become shared. It also does not mean that life is too earnest. There is much for the over 70's to enjoy, and it is worth seeking out others of like mind.

There are, of course, disadvantages. Sight, hearing and suppleness are often casualties of ageing and the body is sometimes prone to aches and pains. The advantages counter all this; to set one's own pace; to think about what one enjoys; to ponder on pleasurable things; to enjoy the company of others who also find humour in a great deal of the world. This book originated from and is indebted to, a very similar group.

You do not have to worry about a mid life crisis.

You are not expected to drive
an articulated lorry.

You can do things when you
want to do them.

You do not have to worry
about investing in a pension.

You can kiss young men
without their wives objecting,
if you are a woman.

You can give
the grandchildren back.

You can sit in any available chair without worrying about giving it up to an old person.

You can start to be proud of your survival strategy.

The great thing about getting older is that you don't lose all the other ages you have been.

You do not need an excuse
to take a nap.

You are not so
likely to be fired.

You can enjoy being plump
as it fills up the wrinkles and
you become more cuddly.

TODAY LIFE IS SO COMPLICATED

So you want to sell me energy services!! Well — presently I have:
- Gas with electric co
- Electric with water co.
- Water with slimline tonic.co
- Telephone with aliens.co
- TV with cafecoco.uk

Hello! Hello! Are you there?

When you are younger,
you get blamed for crimes
you never committed,
and when you are older,
you get credit for virtues
you never possessed.
It evens itself out.

Sometimes you have to wait until the evening to see how glorious the day has been.

It's lovely to let
the youngsters get on
with running the world.
Unravel our mistakes and
then make their own.

Loud blaring music
is not so bad if you can
take your hearing aid out.

One has often outlived
nasty old relatives.

One of the delights known to age, and beyond the grasp of youth, is that of "Not Going".

Opportunity to do
things that one did not
have time for previously.

HARLEY RELIVES
HIS YOUTH

When I dream I am ageless.

YOUNG AT HEART

You do not have to pass an exam to pass the 70 plus.

To me, old age is always fifteen years older than I am.

EVERYONE HAS PROBLEMS
WITH MEMORY AS THEY
GET OLDER